READ FOR FUN

A DAY WITH BRANDY

Ann Mari Falk

Translated by Patricia Crampton
and specially adapted for Stage Two readers
Illustrated by Ilon Wikland

Burke Books LONDON & TORONTO

The rain was drawing streaks on the window.

Peter said, "What awful weather!
I wanted to go out and play with Anne."

Brandy heard him. She wagged her tail
and ran to the door. She wanted to go out too.

Mummy took out a hanky.

"Blow!" she said to Peter, who had streaks, too,
but under his nose, because he had a cold.

"You are not going out," said Mummy.
"And you can't see Anne.
You might give her your cold."

"But I've got nothing to do," said Peter.
"I'm so bored."

"You must have about a hundred things
to play with," said Mummy.

"Think of all your lovely Christmas presents."

"They are not fun any more," said Peter.

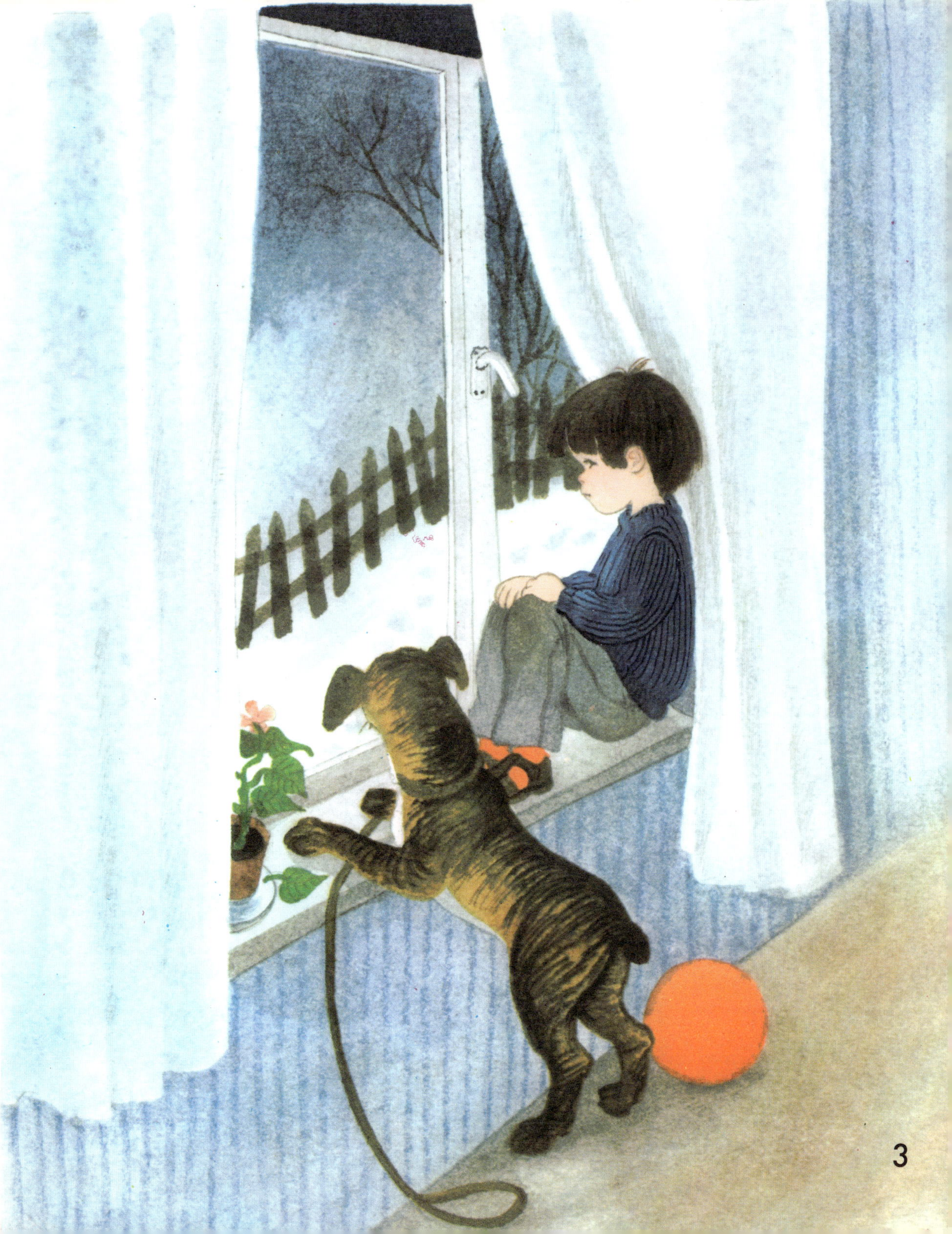

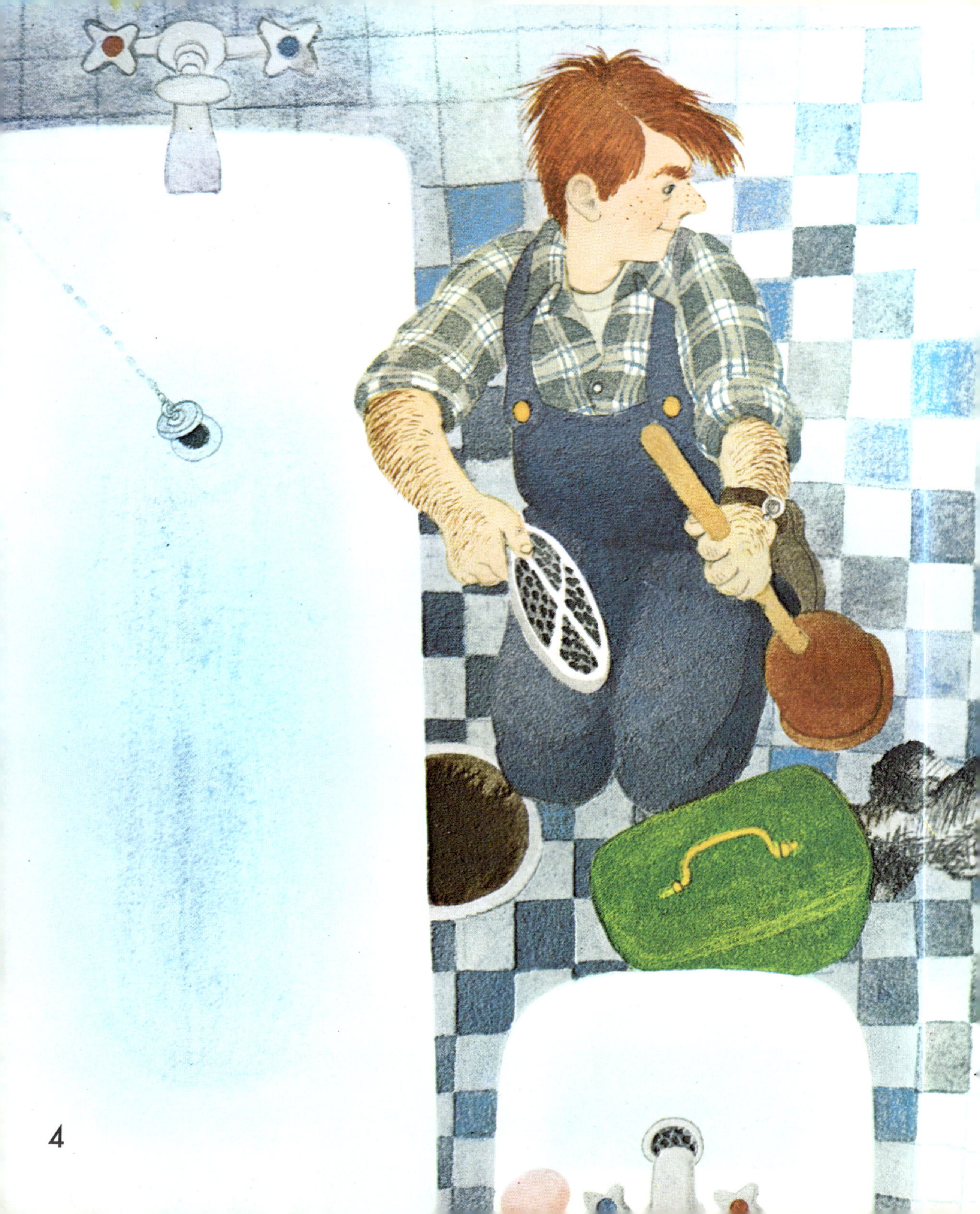

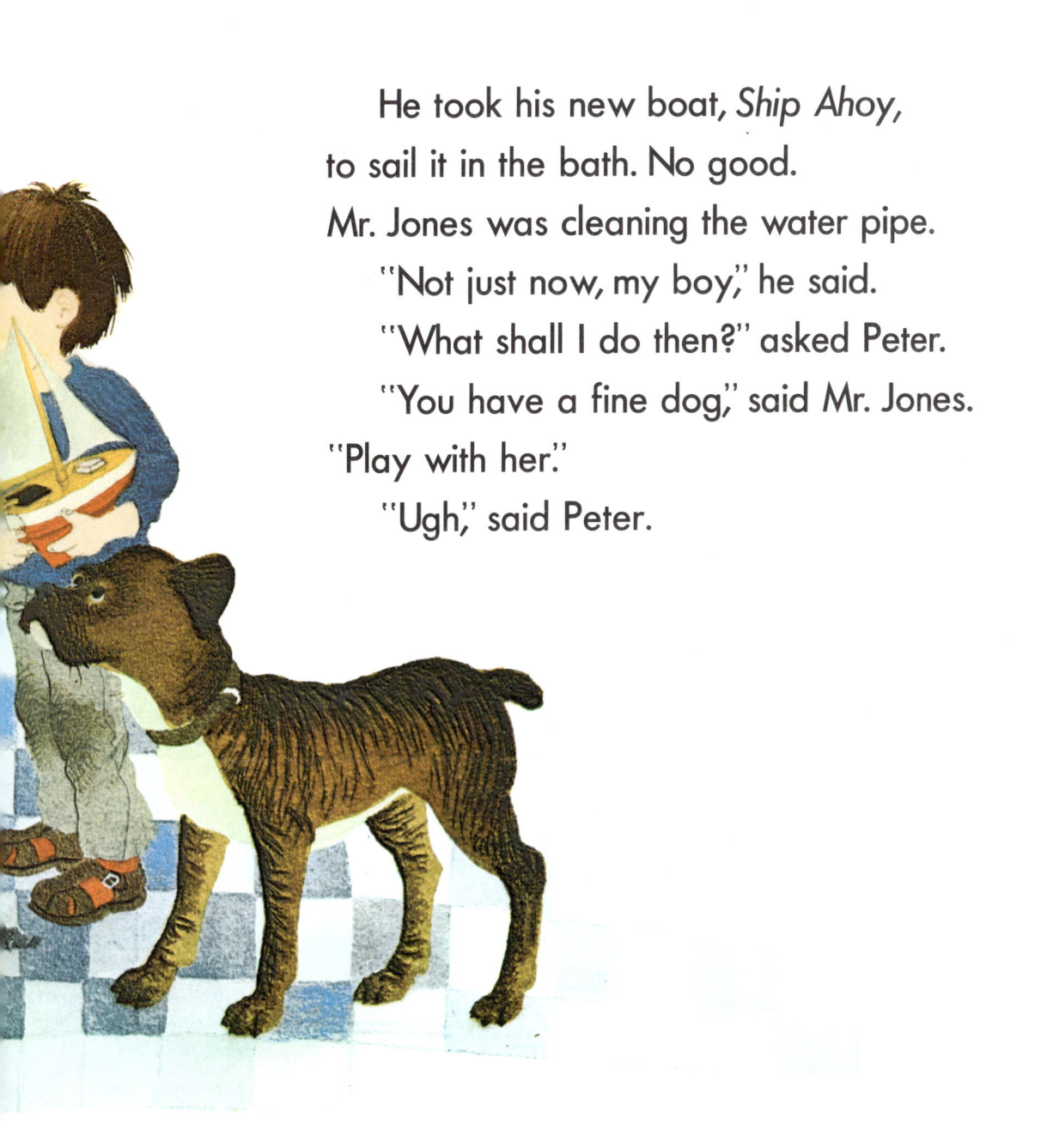

He took his new boat, *Ship Ahoy,*
to sail it in the bath. No good.
Mr. Jones was cleaning the water pipe.

"Not just now, my boy," he said.

"What shall I do then?" asked Peter.

"You have a fine dog," said Mr. Jones.
"Play with her."

"Ugh," said Peter.

Brandy was waiting outside the bathroom. They went down to Mummy in the kitchen.

"I've got nothing to do," said Peter.

"It will soon be lunch time," said Mummy.

Peter took a saucepan from her and put it on his head. He waved the big wooden spoon about.

"I am a policeman", said Peter.

"I am a burglar", said Mr. Jones in a deep voice.

He had come to get a cloth.

Mr. Jones gave Brandy such a fright that she hid under the kitchen table.

"She's not a good police dog," said Peter. "Oh, I'm so bored".

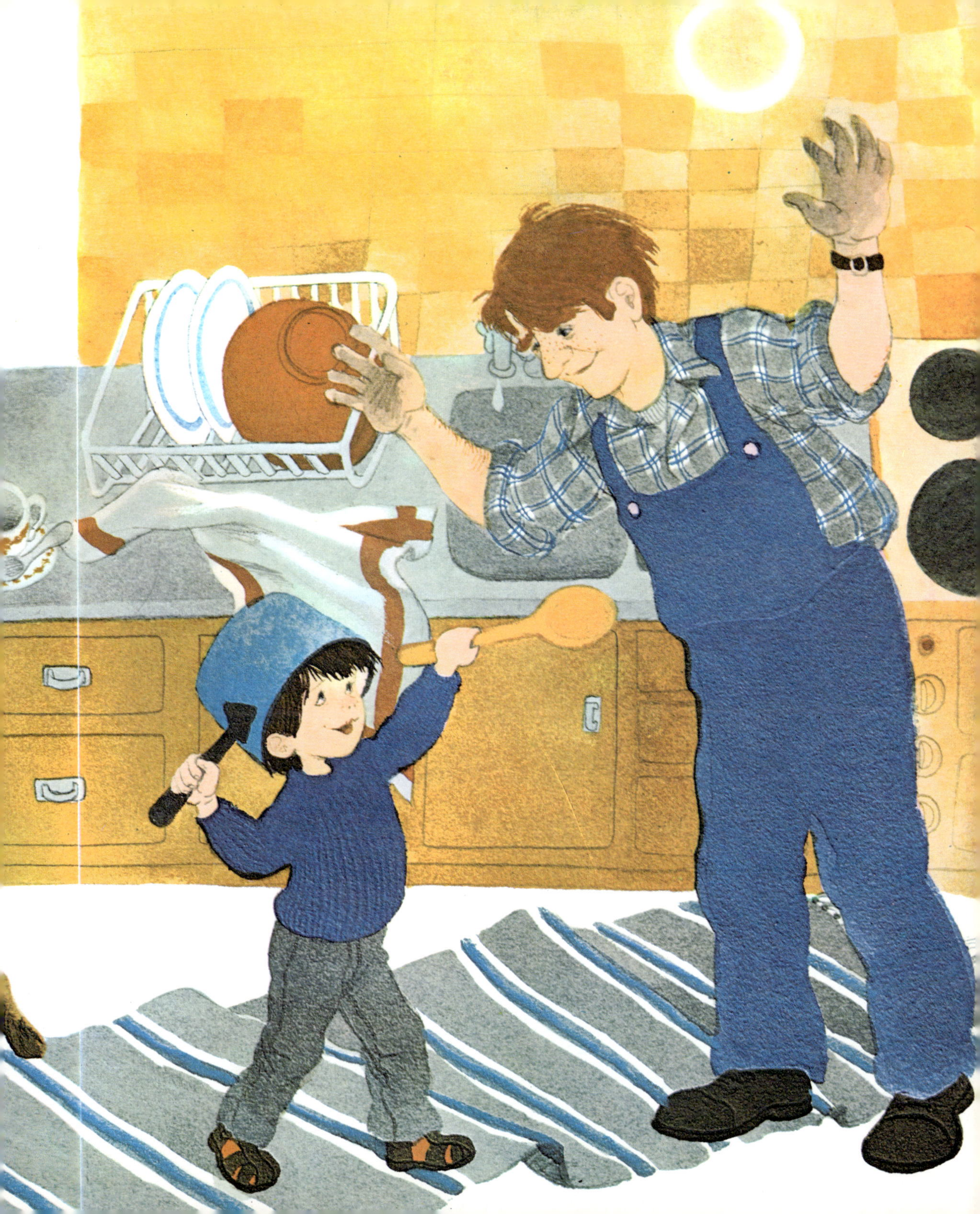

Mummy blew Peter's nose again,
put a big bag on his head
and tied a cloth round his middle.

"Now you are a cook", she said.

"Am I a real cook?" asked Peter.
"Then Brandy and I are going to eat
as much cake and pudding as we like".

"No, thank you", said his mother.
"You would both get a pain".

9

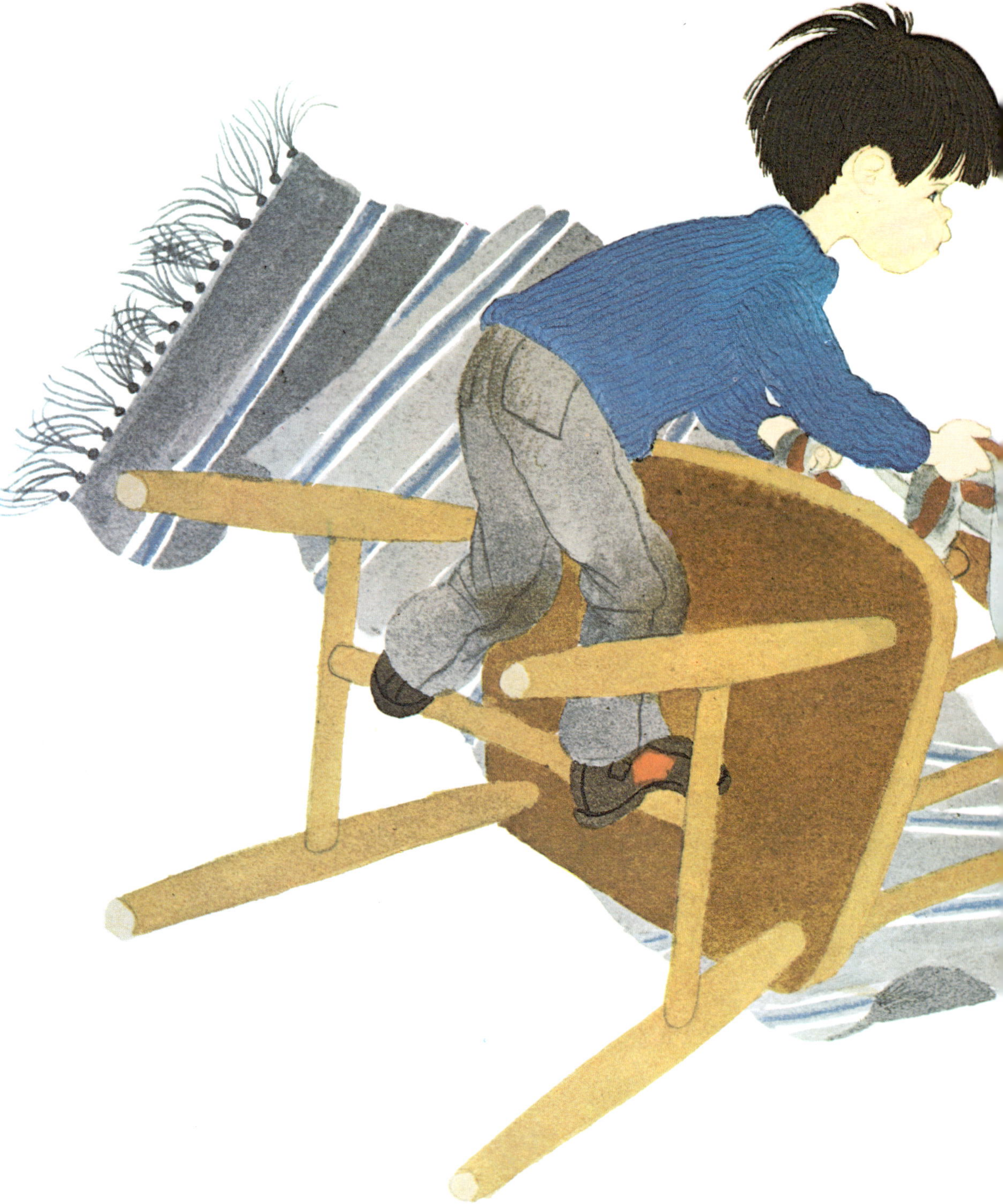

Peter kicked the chair and it fell over.

"What are you doing?" asked Mummy.

"The chair is a cart," said Peter.
"Brandy can pull me."

But Brandy did not want to play horses.
She stayed under the table.

Then Peter took the pancake pan.
The chair which had been a cart
turned into a car
and the pan was a steering-wheel.

Peter tooted and steered.

"Toot toot toot!"

"Driver," called Mummy,
"do you want anything to eat?"

"Of course, I do," said the driver.

"Then I'm sorry," said Mummy,
"but I must have the pan for a minute."

"You're not allowed to,"
said the driver.

"Out of the kitchen, my boy!"
said Mummy. "And Brandy, too."

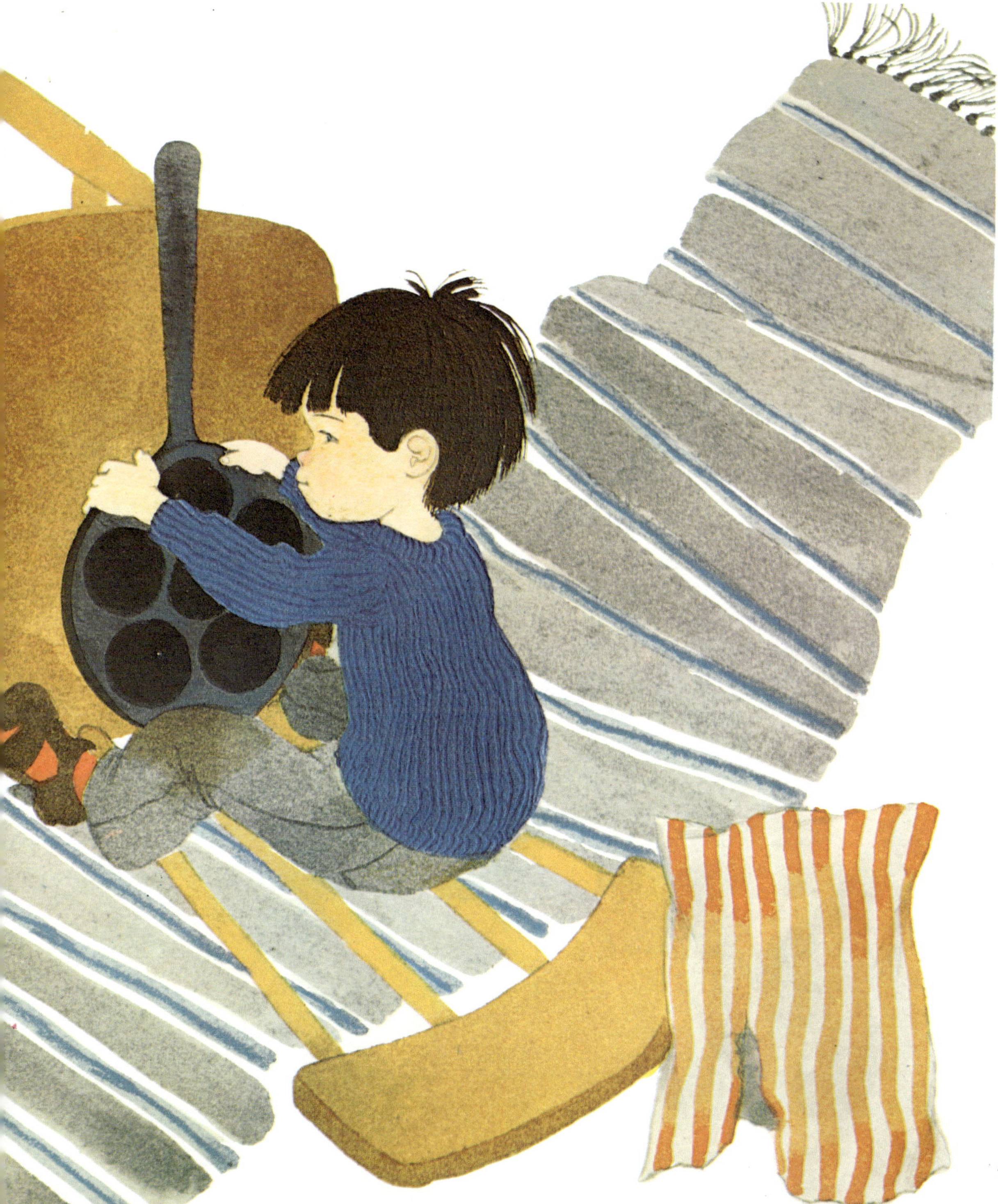

14

Peter and Brandy soon came back.
Peter had Mummy's shoulder bag.
"Good morning," he said.
"I'm the postman."
He held up the letters
and Brandy held up her paw nicely.
Mummy took all the letters.
They were tied up with pink ribbon.
"Put these back, please, Mr. Postman,"
she said.
"No one can have any fun
in this house,"
said the postman.

Brandy licked Peter's hand.

"You are nice," he told her.

"But some people are *not* nice!"

Mr. Jones gave him a pat on the bottom.

"And some people play burglars and steal Mummy's letters," he said.

"But I'm not a burglar," said Peter. He laughed. Brandy showed her teeth as if she were laughing too.

"Here, Brandy," said Peter. "We will go now."

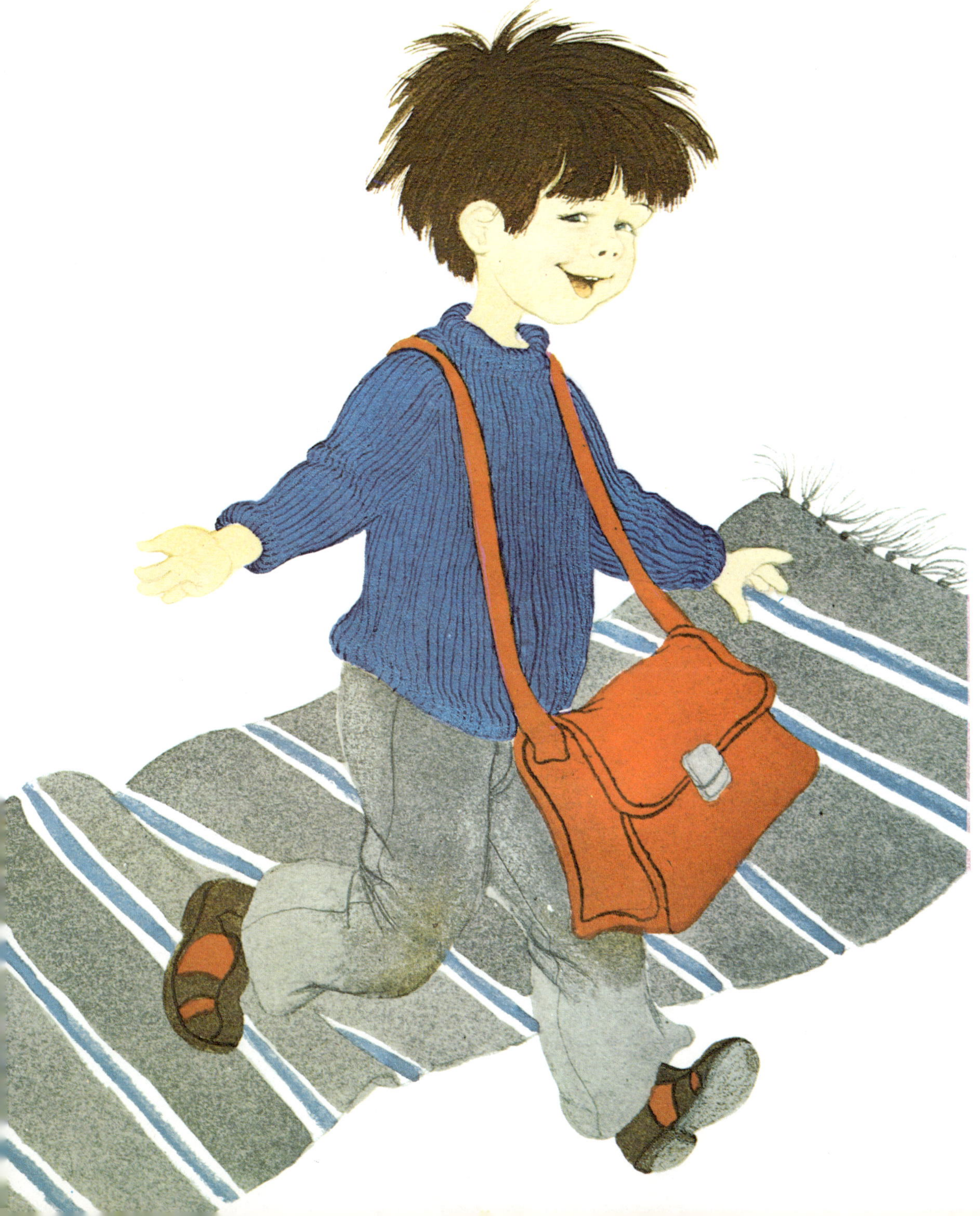

18

Mummy made pancakes. Mr. Jones mended the tap.
Then this awful pirate ran into the room.
He had a black patch over one eye,
Mummy's scarf on his head
and gold curtain rings in his ears.

"Brandy is the ship's dog," he said.

"But Brandy does not like water," said Mummy
and she laughed.

That made the pirate very cross.

"Oh, I'm so bored," he said.
"I've got nothing to do."

Mr. Jones said, "When I was little
I wanted to be Father Christmas,
because he only has to work once a year!"

Mr. Jones said goodbye. Mummy made pancakes.
Then she nearly dropped the pan
because the door opened
and a white ghost cried,
"Woo-hoo-hoo!"

It was Brandy who saved Mummy and the pan.
She jumped round the ghost and pulled.
There! A sheet was lying on the floor.

"Oh, it's my own little boy!"
said Mummy, kissing Peter.
"I really thought I had seen a ghost."

A little later, Daddy came home from work.
Then they all sat round the table.
They ate lots of pancakes and jam.
Mummy had cooked potato and liver for Brandy.

"What kind of day have you had?" asked Daddy.

"Boring," said Peter, with his mouth full.

Just then there was a ring at the door.
Peter and Brandy ran to open it.

There was Anne.
She had a pink scarf
and a red nose.

"I have a cold, too,"
she said.
"So I can play with you,
after all."

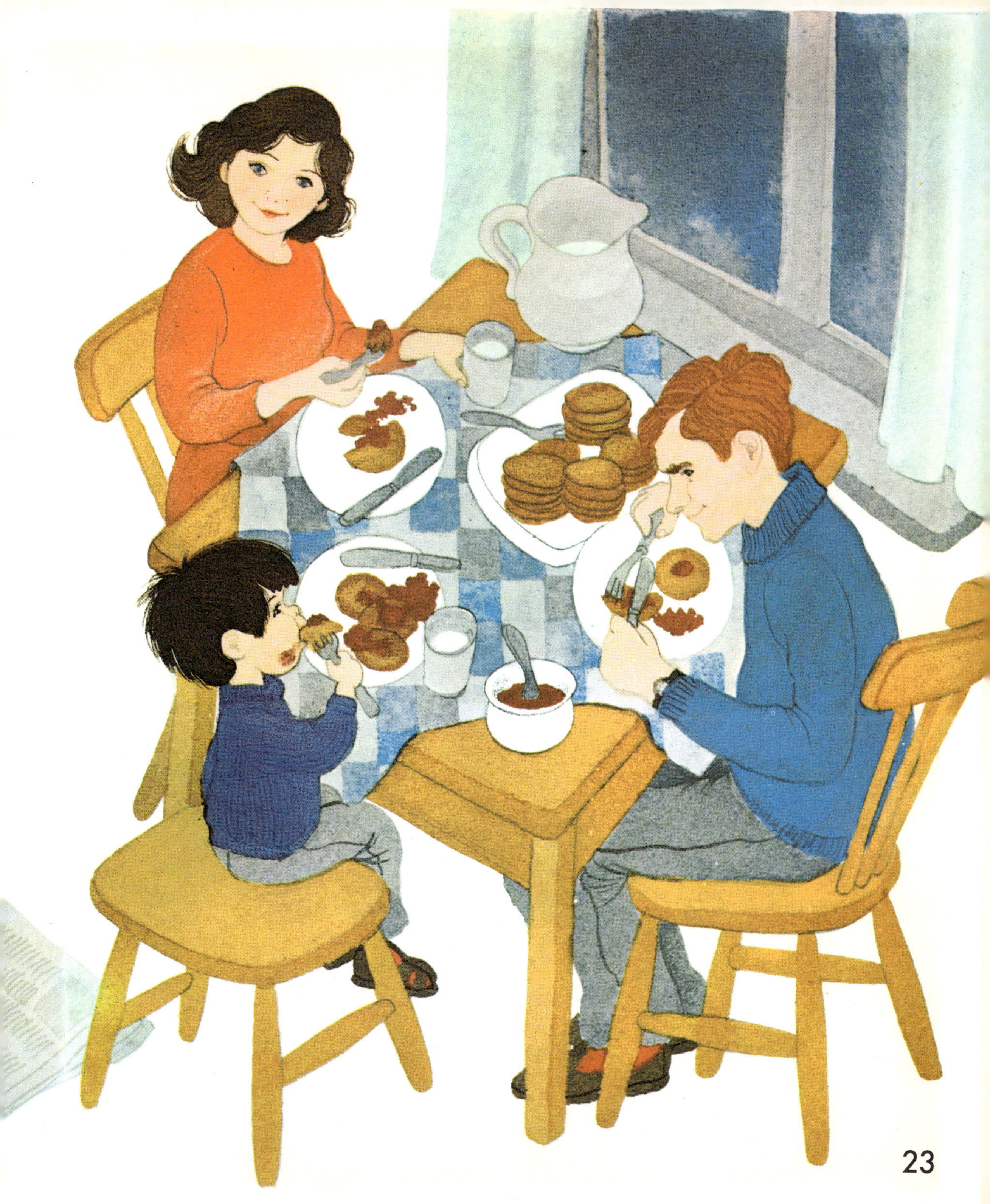

TRANSLATED AND ADAPTED FROM
"KOM OCH LEK, RUFFA"
© ANN MARI FALK 1972
THIS TRANSLATION FIRST PUBLISHED AUGUST 1975
© BURKE PUBLISHING COMPANY LIMITED 1975
ILLUSTRATIONS © ILON WIKLAND 1972

All rights reserved. No part of this publication may be reproduced, stored in a retrieval system, or transmitted, in any form or by any means, electronic, mechanical, photocopying, recording or otherwise, without the prior permission of Burke Publishing Company Limited or Burke Publishing (Canada) Limited.

ISBN	0	222	00340	5	Hardbound
ISBN	0	222	00344	8	Limp
ISBN	0	222	00336	7	Library

BURKE PUBLISHING COMPANY LIMITED, 14 JOHN STREET, LONDON WC1N 2EJ.
BURKE PUBLISHING (CANADA) LIMITED, P.O. BOX 48, TORONTO-DOMINION CENTRE, TORONTO 111, ONTARIO.
PRINTED IN GREAT BRITAIN BY
WILLIAM CLOWES & SONS, LIMITED, LONDON, BECCLES AND COLCHESTER